From CREEPIN – 2 – PREACHIN

Renee R. White

From CREEPIN — 2 — PREACHIN

Renee R. White

Charleston, SC
www.PalmettoPublishing.com

From Creepin 2 Preachin
Copyright © 2023 by Renee R. White

All rights reserved

All photos are from Moving In Motion by Mac, LLC

No portion of this book may be reproduced, stored in a retrieval system, or transmitted in any form by any means–electronic, mechanical, photocopy, recording, or other–except for brief quotations in printed reviews, without prior permission of the author.

Paperback ISBN: 979-8-8229-1700-2
eBook ISBN: 979-8-8229-1701-9

Dedication

This book is dedicated to my first love, the one who is and who is to come.

Table of Contents

Dedication · v
Preface · 1
Tigers · 3
Kaloramo · 4
Easter Sunday and Easter Monday · 4
Roots · 6
The Rec · 6
Bad Bad Bad Bully · 7
Upward Bound · 7
Stick and Move · 8
Childhood Gone too Soon · 8
Rough Riders · 9
Chuck Baby · 10
Hustler's Ball · 10
We going out tonight · 11
Hungover · 11
Tis the Season · 12
DMV Girlfriend · 12
Baptism · 13
Prom Night · 13
It's a Boy · 13
What's in a name · 14
Keep Away From It Welfare · 14
Time with Baby Boy · 15
I Scream, You Scream, We All Scream for Ice Cream · 15
UDC & Parent Child Center · 16
J.o.b. · 16
Ho-Ho-Ho · 17
My Cross to Bare · 17
You're Dating Who · 18
Far Too Many Games that People Play · 19

Brainwashed · 19
I look better going than I did coming · · · · · · · · · · · · · · · · · · · 20
Second Time Around Not A Charm · · · · · · · · · · · · · · · · · · · 20
Ma Don't Leave Me Here · 20
Crying and Dying Inside · 22
No Show · 22
T-19 · 22
My Rock · 23
Layers of Me · 23
Convicted · 24
Go! · 25
Why Me! · 26
Jesus on the line · 26
Preachin' Time · 27
About the Author: · 29

Preface

I was born on November 9 in the late 1960s after the DC riots at DC General Hospital to a loving mom. My parents weren't married, so I was what they called a love child, or bastard. I was the third of four siblings and frisky. I grew up in an area of DC known was Uptown (Northwest).

Living at 1450 we had a childhood a kid can only imagine. We lived on the block where everybody knew everybody, and if the neighbor saw you doing something, they would call your parents after they addressed the issue.

My granny was known for her parties and entertainment. She was the matriarch of the family. (PS: She didn't take no mess.) Granny was known for her cooking. Daily, she cooked breakfast, lunch, and dinner. She fed anyone who wanted a meal. It would be no surprise to be eating dinner with the local neighborhood alcoholic.

Christmas season was big at 1450. My family did it big. Our Christmas tree would go as high as the ceiling with lots of toys underneath. One Christmas my oldest brother who was always a prankster played a trick on me. Our room faced the street so we could see all the toys and gifts coming in and out of the house. My brother was looking outside the window and saw our uncle bringing bikes inside the house.

My brother said, "Uncle has one bike for me and one bike for my sister, and Renee, you don't have a bike."

But I did. Between my mom and her brothers, they spoiled us. We got whatever we asked for and even more. I was a small pint, but I had a weekly routine every Saturday. I walked to the Giant around the corner and grabbed a box of Fruity Pebbles and a gallon of milk and then jumped onto the moving carousel which took me outside the store. I walked back home to watch my favorite cartoons in front of the floor model TV.

As a little kid I was so curious about fire. One day while home with Ma before I started attending school, I was playing with matches and lit a pile of clothing. The fire scared me, and I ran into Ma's room and hid under the covers. Ma woke and opened the door to a ball of flames. She grabbed me and jumped down the steps and ran outside with me in her arms. That was my first time but not my only time burning down the house.

Tigers

Unfortunately, it was time for me to attend school. I really enjoyed watching my siblings go to school while I stayed at home with Ma. My first-grade teacher was nice, but I would cry daily to go home. So, Ma would come and pick me up. She told me that I needed to stop acting like a little baby. But I never grew out of it. First grade came and I had to repeat the grade. My main problem was I didn't want to leave Ma. Attending school didn't come easy for me, until the third grade when I'met my best friend. She lived just up the street from me, but we were always together. Then I met another friend of ours and she lived around the corner from me as well. We would walk to school together all the time.

My girlfriends made attending school fun. They made good grades, so I started making good grades as well. One day while walking home from school a little girl wanted to fight me. So, the crowd placed a stick on my shoulder and one on her shoulder. She said to me, "I dare you to knock my mother off my shoulder."

So, I did. We fought that day and many days after. A few years later we both joined the safety patrol, but we only wanted to march in the annual Safety Patrol Parade. We both knew that by marching in that parade everybody we see us, and we would be able to show off our uniforms. We were about to march, and we looked stunned with our white shirts and white pants with white shoes. We were stepping.

I would sum up my years of grammar school as boring until I joined the street cheerleaders. This team was made up of girls who lived within my block, and we formed a team. The team would compete with other girls outside of our area where we battled in your face and where I mastered the art of cussing. We were the best team and we won battles all the time.

I recall when my mom first heard me cuss. We were battling the Shepard Street Team and they were going to win the battle, but I came out and went toe-to-toe with another girl and my mom heard my vulgar language. We won the battle, but I lost my mom's thoughts of my youthful innocence.

Kaloramo

Saturday night was skate night. Weekly, everyone around the block went down to Kaloramo skating rink to skate and listen to the organ and just hang out with friends. It was like family every weekend. We would skate and hang out and meet. Skating was the best activity ever. Until one day it ended. But we still have the memories.

Easter Sunday and Easter Monday

This was my best time of the year when the weather was nice, and spring was in the air. Whenever Easter came around, we would walk down to the end of the block to our hairstylist Ms. Barbara. She was on Fourteenth Street.

Ms. Barbara would do my hair and my sister's hair. We both got press and curl but for me it was not a pleasant event. I am so tender headed, and this is something I never grew out of. But I thought that Ms. Barbara just burned me all the time with those straightener combs. She would take her time back in my kitchen area.

Nevertheless, I would love the end results and we would take pictures once we put on our Sunday Best. After church we would have a big dinner. But on the Easter Monday it was lights, camera, action at the National Zoo. Everybody from all parts of DC would meet at the zoo as it is a tradition in DC. We would just be walking around not seeing the animals but just looking at what others were wearing.

When I was around ten years old, we moved to 1505. Things changed once we got down there. We had a new addition to the family: my youngest brother.

Since I was around six or seven, my godfather would come pick me up and take me to church. I stayed in church from sunrise to sunset. When I became a teen, I said no more church. This was the time when my granny begins to travel more with the Eastern Stars. When she traveled that meant that Ma had to cook for us. My

Ma was not really fond of cooking, although she had her favorite dishes, such as hot dogs and beans or hot dogs and spaghetti. We loved Ma but her cooking was not so great. We were just spoiled from granny cooking. We were so spoiled that we made a song every time she left. "We really miss you Grannnnnyyyy..." We sang it every time she left.

Roots

I loved traveling with Ma. One time we traveled down to North Carolina. During my visit I had such a good time. While we were heading back home, I felt so sick, my eyes were yellow, and my stomach hurt. My mom called my granny, and she told her to get me back home. My granny told me later that someone placed roots on me (satanic attack).

The Rec

When I was in junior high school, I decided to join the cheerleader team at the local recreation center at Lincoln. I was already a street cheerleader where we would battle cheerleaders within our local blocks. This kind of cheerleader was loud and in your face. But I loved it.

We would have battled every weekend at the triangle, which was our home turf. Teams from all around the DC area would come to battle us and we would win every time. But of course, you win so much one day you will fall, and we did we fell hard. I don't like to talk about what happened, but to say the least it was Dallas and The Washington Team. So, so sad. That was my last time street cheering. I started focusing more on my team at the rec. This team had uniforms and coordination. Jumps and flips and no cussing. We would go with the basketball team to different schools and cheer, and it was so much fun.

Bad Bad Bad Bully

I was the only seventh grader with gold chains and gold earrings. A new school year began, and I was attending the seventh grade and a new school. My first day I walked through the halls with all my gold chains and gold earrings and a pair of Etienne Aigner riding boots. I thought I was the cat's meow.

It was then that I was approached by a bully. She came up to me and snatched all the jewelry off my neck. I was shocked and started crying and ran to find my brother. Once I told my brother what had happened, he told me that I was going to fight her at three o'clock. I couldn't even focus all day during class, I was so afraid of what could happen to me at three o'clock.

Once three o'clock arrived, everyone was out at the basketball court waiting for me to arrive. We fought, and I must declare I didn't enjoy it at all; it felt forced. I never enjoyed fighting. It wasn't my thing at all. Years later I apologized to her for my behavior, and she accepted.

Upward Bound

Next, I attended Lincoln Junior High School and was a recreation cheerleader. My grades in school were on point and I stayed on the honor roll. My best friend and I got accepted in the Howard University's Upward Bound program. But little did anyone know I was pregnant and was heading to the clinic that weekend. That was the first of many abortions to come.

This program allows you to attend college classes, stay on campus during the summer months, and earn credit toward a college degree. College was fun. My friend and I met kids from other schools within the DMV. We had an annual trip and they decided to take us to Disney World in Florida. My best friend and I had a ball. We rented mopeds (which we couldn't ride), and we rode around the park. I fell on the moped and it burn my right leg. I never rode again.

During the summer months we would stay-on campus because most of the students go back home. My best friend and I would have a blast playing with this foam pointer finger. We played our tricks carefully; we would wait until people started studying and would go from room and room with the pointer. It was hilarious. It still makes me laugh to this day.

Stick and Move

My first boyfriend was a boxer, and I was his best opponent. At the age of fourteen I had my first pregnancy. By the age of sixteen I had three abortions. I had a boyfriend; at least he claimed me for years. We had daily fighting matches and we fought from Fourteenth Parkwood to Fourteenth and Swan Street. Sometimes it would end well and sometimes it wouldn't. But what could I say? He had given me everything I wanted.

Even though he gave me everything there were times when things really got bad. After my abortion, we broke up and during the break-up I met this really nice guy. I met him during eighth grade at Lincoln and we were voted Best Couple of the Year. What people didn't know was when we took that picture for the yearbook, I was pregnant. Yes, I was pregnant in the eighth grade.

Childhood Gone too Soon

Since I started dating early, I thought why not start hanging out. My first club experience was on Thirteenth and Upshur Street at the

ClubHouse. I was only fourteen years old, with heels and a white jumpsuit, it worked. Compliments to the glam squad (my sister).

Rough Riders

I attended Theodore Roosevelt High School from the ninth grade to the twelfth grade. One day I was walking to school I had on a Jordache jean jacket and a pair of white K-Swiss tennis shoes. I was looking for so fly walking to Roosevelt. Little did I know my ex-boyfriend was following me once I bent the corner it was on. He snatched the jacket and made me take off my K-Swiss sneakers. I came back home barefooted, and my granny said, "I hope you learned your lesson."

But I didn't. We made up later on and this happened off and on for the next five years. I recall a time when I got pregnant, and I went down to the clinic located on Seventeenth and Q Street. My ex-boyfriend at the time met me down there after my procedure and we fought all the way back to 1505. He was known by many people, and I enjoyed our time together when we weren't fighting. My oldest uncle told my mom that this guy was too old for me and no good. (That was the truth.) Once I went down to King's Dominion to a summer concert with my sister and her friends. Guess what? He was down there ready to start a fight.

I can recall when we broke up and I went to the concert with a guy I met, and the ex-showed up and showed off. He scared the boy away from me and that was the end of our relationship. I didn't want to be with him anymore so I stopped being around him, but he would always show up and start trouble. We grew apart and I finally was able to begin a life without being an opponent, or so I thought.

Chuck Baby

I loved Go-go music so weekly we went down to Howard Theater to hear Chuck Brown and the Soul Searchers. It was a tradition to go down to 9th Street and hang out at the Howard Theater weekly. If I wasn't at the Howard, I would be the court on 14th street. We would follow bands all over DC. EU, Backyard, Rare Essence and of course the man of the hour Chuck Brown and the Soul Searchers. Go-Go was in my blood and going to the go-go you had to be fly with the latest gear all the time. I really enjoyed dancing on the balcony of the Howard. Bands use to play at high schools all around DC and I tried to make as many as possible except southeast. Then the Howard closed and my club life began. I would hit up the Ibex, Ritz, and my favorite, Kilimanjaro. I enjoyed house music and it drove me wild and I would leave the club with my hair stuck to my head. Most of these club had guy with job but I didn't trust working men; I was only attracted to bad boys. My uncle had a saying. He would say, "Renee can you please stop standing beside the jailhouse?"

Hustler's Ball

There was an event every year called Hustler's Ball. We would go down to Adean's and get my hair done then go to White Flint for an outfit. This event brought everybody out who was somebody. This event was held at the convention center annually. You would see the best of the best outfits. We would go just to be seen and listen to good music and to see who was there. It's a DC thing; outsiders wouldn't understand. We dressed to impress.

We going out tonight

I only dated hustlers and what they drove and what they wore was a matter of importance for me. I despised the working man. I remember having six companions at one time. I met a guy and things changed from there. We would hang out every day after I left work. He would take me shopping at Lord & Taylor at White Flint Mall. I had no limit and things were looking really, good. Until my ex boyfriend showed up and things would change. He thought of me as his wife, and I was only a teenager. I recall a time when we had broken up and I went to a Luther Vandross show with another guy. I was dressed to the nines. I was so fly. But as soon as I hit that door, I saw him, and I know trouble was lurking. On that night he approached me I ignored him and stay with my new friend but that didn't work for long. He started making comments about him and how he was going to knock him out. The night ended with me riding home with the sister and her friends.

Hungover

After a long night listening to Chuck at the Howard Theater we would wake up hungry. So we came up with a ritual every Saturday morning. My sister and her best friend would ask me to wake granny up so we could eat a good breakfast. You see, every Saturday was clean-up day. We cleaned the house from top to bottom. But in order for us to get granny to cook we had to clean, and we were so tired that I had to help with the cooking so that we all could eat before we clean. This would happen whenever we went out to the Go-go.

Tis the Season

Christmas time at 1505 was so different than 1450 we started a new tradition where we would all go to the Uptown Movie Theater to see the latest blockbuster release. After the movies we would go down to the Ice-Skating Ring on 9th Street, NW. (PS: I still maintain that tradition today with my grandkids.)

On one Christmas my uncle opened up all the gifts under the tree. (He was torn up). Once we will wake up, my uncle told all of us whose gifts they were. My mom was so mad. Once all turned teenagers, my uncle would place envelopes on the fireplace with money inside. Oh yeah, money was better than gifts.

DMV Girlfriend

I was the DMV girlfriend and respect for my body was not important for me at that time. My motivation was as long as I was wearing a fly outfit I would stay in the in game. Of course, I had birth control pills, but I didn't take them and when I did, I took them all at once.

When high school came around, I slowed down, and I got serious about school started going back to church. I had a steady boyfriend and my grades improved. One Sunday morning while getting dressed to go to church, I asked my granny to zip my skirt. My granny said, " that it won't fit because you are pregnant." I cried because I thought I was changing for the better.

Later that day she called my dad to tell him the news and as soon as I heard his voice I began to cry. He sounded so disappointed with me. He said something to me that was shocking. He mentioned Romans 3:23, "For all have sinned and fallen short of the glory of God." Little did he know how that scripture would apply to what I have going on right now.

Baptism

The following Sunday I went up to the altar and gave my life to Christ was baptized that following Saturday. After my baptism I felt so much pressure at church as a teen mom from the ladies at the church. The rumors were that I had a baby out of wedlock. The people would look at me as if I was a disease. I left the church. But I would later regard that decision.

Prom Night

During my senior year of high school, I got pregnant, and I decided to keep it because I had already had two previous abortions behind me. I knew I had to change my game, so I got a stay-in-school job.

This job would allow me to go to school and still work and save money. I did attend the prom at Omni Shore Hotel near Calvert Street Bridge, and I had a great time. On June 3, 1986, this night I was extremely nervous because I had to walk across the stage to obtain my high school degree. I had a dream that my water would break while I was walking across the stage. Thanks to many prayers, I was able to strut across the stage with my son in my tummy at graduation in DARS Constitution Hall.

It's a Boy

On that Sunday morning, I walked into Ma's room and told her that I couldn't stop peeing. She told me that my water broke and drove me to Washington Adventist Hospital. My son was breach, so the nurse told me that they had to turn him around. That little sucker had me in labor from 7:00 a.m. until 11:58 p.m. My son was a six-pound, three-ounce and twenty-one inches long. I whispered to him, "Mommy loves you." I knew then that I would do whatever it took to make his life much better than mine. He was so hairy I couldn't even see his eyes, but he smiled, and then my heart melted. After the birth of my son, I saw how hairy he was and how long of a baby he was. I also noticed that he had hair all over his face and down his back. I laid there counting all his toes and fingers to make sure nothing was missing. My son kept his eyes tightly closed but all of a sudden, my sister spoke, and he stuck his tongue out at her. My mom was overjoyed he was her second grandchild.

What's in a name

My son's dad asked me to do him a favor and name him after him, so I did. My relationship with him faded away shortly after my birth of my son. I didn't have much patience with him he couldn't find employment, so I just had to make a decision for us both.

Keep Away From It Welfare

Once I dropped out my mom said OKAY, now it is time for you to get a job. It took me about a few months, but I got a job. Because the thought of going on welfare was so depressing for me. But I did try. I caught the bus downtown to the welfare department and met with one of the social workers. When I met with the social worker, she began to ask me questions about my son's father and where he lives and what kind of work he does. I sat there, and all I saw was Diahann Carroll in Claudine; it was the scene when the social worker came over, and she had to hide all the items her boyfriend purchased for her, and she also had to answer some demeaning questions. Oh, no, that was not for this kid. I'm out!

Once I left her office, I caught the first thing smoking back uptown. I got off at Marie Reed Recreation Center. I heard about this new program for women, infants, and children, called WIC. I was allowed to sign up, and they gave me vouchers to purchase milk, cereal, and other necessary items for my son. I stayed on that program until he was five years old. It was the best program ever.

Time with Baby Boy

It was the most precious time and the most challenging time. I was so broke that I would tell my son that we would have a new adventure. The adventure was we would spend time at the local library. We would walk up to the Meridian Hill Library on Sixteenth Street: my son, my nephew, and me. While walking with my son and my nephew, we would take in the sights. We would walk down Sixteenth Street and make a right onto Newton Street, then a right onto Brown Street. Times were so hard. We would walk right by Little Giant's, and I would smell those juicy hamburgers but had no money to purchase one. Then we walked by my favorite spot of all time, Heller's Bakery. I made sure that I had enough to make that stop. We would spend hours in the library reading different books then it was time to make the stop at Heller's Bakery and get two cupcakes for them. I only had five dollars to make the purchase, but to see their faces made my heart glad.

I Scream, You Scream, We All Scream for Ice Cream

I once held a job at the Air & Space Museum for less than six short months. This position was selling ice cream on the carts. But what people didn't know was I was only working to saving up money to go the Frankie Beverly and Maze Show at the Convention Center on Seventh Street. Once I got my money straight, I caught a bus to White Flint Mall to purchase a mustard linen suit from I. Magnum.

UDC & Parent Child Center

Ma and my uncle came up with a plan for me to finish college so they would watch my son while I attended school. I decided to enroll in UDC for some college courses. The campus reminded me high school everyone knows everybody it was so much fun. I didn't have time to apply myself to my courses. I met a friend, and he was really nice. He lived on W Street. We dated for a little while; his mom worked at the daycare. Through him I was able to get a job at the daycare. I got a job as a receptionist, and my son was able to attend for free. During these times W Street was hot with addicts and so much activity going on daily. I would walk through a crowd of people just to get to Dottie's to get something to eat. The daycare allowed me to work while my son take advantage of the programs they offered for free. Once I left the daycare, we stopped dating.

J.o.b.

I stayed at the daycare for two years, and then I applied for a new job at the DC jail as a clerk. This was my most adventurous job ever. The job gave me a sense of purpose.

While working for Classification and Parole I performed the task of parole and sentence computation of inmates. On some occasions I would be detailed at the Marshall Cell Block to process releases from the court. I stayed at the jail for about eight years, then it was time for a new adventure. I got a job working as an administrative assistant to a famous basketball player. My time there was short lived as I didn't gel with my boss, so I left the firm. I then decided to work for a security company. I rose through the ranks from private to captain in just two years. I was in charge of all the NationsBank within the DMV. This position allowed me to accept the position as a Project Manager at a luxury hotel in downtown DC. Once I finished that contract, I decided I needed real employment, so I applied to Washington Hospital Center where I only stayed for two years. During my employment at WHC I met a really good friend of mine. One day she told me about a position that she was applying for at the Library of Congress we both got hired. Then our journey began, which led to present day.

Ho-Ho-Ho

I remember sleeping here and there not using protection. I recall when my son was six months old, I got pregnant. On that Saturday I went to the clinic on Pennsylvania Avenue. I got an abortion and the doctor said to me, "I think something else was there."
   On that Monday I had a real bad stomach cramp that sent me to the emergency room of Washington Hospital Center. While at the hospital the nurse examined me, then ran out the room. Shortly after, she returned with the team of doctors. The doctors said that you need to have emergency surgery right now. The doctor turned the sonogram monitor around for me and I saw something inside my Fallopian tube. Well, to my surprise, it was a baby. Which would cause me to die if it was not removed. They gave me a bikini cut my first scar east to west. By the age of twenty-one I had five abortions and one birth.

My Cross to Bare

Nine years later I had an obstruction inside my large intestines that was the north to south scar. What happened was for about over a week I had no bowel movements, so my stomach was cramping. Once again, I found myself inside the ER of Washington Hospital Center. Inside, the ER the nurse tried to examine me, but I wouldn't allow her to touch me because my stomach was so sensitive. Needless to say, the exam was performed. What they found caused a crowd of doctors to come in and speak with me. This time the head doctor asks me to call my family before they would discuss what is happening. Upon arrival of my family, the doctors came in and spoke with Ma and told her that they found a foot of my intestine blocked. This blockage was causing me to not have any bowel movements. The doctor ask does anyone in the family has the same blood type in case we need it during the surgery. My youngest brother had the same blood type, but I told him no. I stayed in the hospital for several days. Upon my departure I had yellow jaundice. Finally, I gave up the street. No more whoring around. I needed employment because I had a son and I wanted to live to see him become a man. While in the hospital, I was visited by one of the possible fathers who told me that the baby wasn't his and never mentioned that I was pregnant by him to anyone. Once I came home, another friend of mine came to the house with balloons and flowers, but I had to tell him that the baby was gone, and we were done.

You're Dating Who

I grew up with my ex-husband on Newton Street. He is my oldest brother's best friend. We all grew up on the same block, and our families are so intertwined still to this day. We played hide and seek and 1-2-3-4 red light. Our block was the "it" block. All the kids in the area stayed on our block we had fun all the time. Our relationship was reckless to say the least. We started dating when my son was only four years old. We moved in on U Street. After a few years of dating, we decided to take it to the next level and get married. We got married at DC Superior Court. My mother was so upset that she saw something which I couldn't see myself. I took my son and myself though physical and mental hell for many years. We moved at least six times, and my son attended three elementary schools and two junior high schools, so once he got to the high school level, he said to me, "Ma, please can I please go to one high school?" So, he did. He went to the big castle on the hill, a.k.a. Cardozo.

Far Too Many Games that People Play

I got married at the age of twenty-three after my ex husband did a bid in jail that marriage was a rollercoaster so many ups and downs. We fought about money, other women, lying, and him not keeping a job. We lived in DC most of the time, then we moved to Maryland.

One Saturday while hanging out with my brother we went to Georgetown for dinner at Uno Pizzeria. While leaving the restaurant I saw him (the husband) driving with another female in the car. I quickly ran toward the car and grabbed the handle and snatched it off. He pulled off while I had the door handle in my hand. Later on, that night we had a huge fight. I left and went to my mom's but came back days later. This abuse went on for twenty years, but as time went by, It was more at risk.

Brainwashed

Religion was his way of controlling me, and for years I complied to his demands. I must admit I was totally brainwashed by the husband. He introduced me to a religion, which was Jehovah's Witness. I began to attend the Kingdom Hall with him and my son. We attended together for a while then he stopped attending with us. I was still practicing the religion for years and studied and attended conventions yearly. The husband used this religion to control me, and I didn't see any way out. I was all in, and so I just stayed. I never got baptized because I didn't agree with them calling Jesus a prophet. Years later I had an aha moment, and I stopped attending all meeting and studying.

I look better going than I did coming

I finally got tired and decided to leave after nearly twenty years of blood, sweat, and tears. I am the kind of person who wanted my marriage to work, so after the first marriage we spent six years apart and came back for a second round. We decided that we couldn't date each other so we got married again. But something changed in me. I had grown. I wanted to make it work again so I went back for unfinished business.

Second Time Around Not A Charm

The second time was a charm, so I thought. This time it only took six years and one regretful night to make me cut my loses. This time we did leave on bad terms. It was about two years later when the divorce was finalized, and we met again. I wanted to apologize to the husband for any problems which I caused within the marriage. He didn't know that we were divorced because he didn't show for court, but I advised him. During our second time I was warned by so many people, but I didn't heed the warnings.

Ma Don't Leave Me Here

My mom passed in September of 2002 right after 9/11. She was the miniature rock in the family because granny was the big rock. But with two of them they make a quarry, which was all of us. I can remember I received a call from my nephew. My nephew said that he called DC Ambulance to the house because ma was feeling well. I had just left work and came home at the time I left Southwest DC. My mind was racing and had to hit the park before the Rock Creek Park changed to inbound traffic.

So, I made it to 1505, and my ma was talking with the paramedic, and she was telling them that she had just left the hospital and that she was having trouble breathing. They examined her, and her vitals were a little high. The paramedics decided to take transport her to the Washington Hospital Center. I told them I would meet them there. I was the only kid there with my ma for hours, so we talked, and she asked me why I was working so hard and as if I was up to something.

I told her no, but what I should have told her was yes, I was trying to get a house. If I would have known that would have been my last conversation with Ma, I wish I would have told her so much more. I left the hospital once my sister and father-in-law came. I went home to get sleep, and I believed that things would be alright.

About a few hours later I received a phone call from my father-in-law. He told me to get back to the hospital because Ma had taken a turn for the worse. Once I arrived, I went straight back to the ER where she was. I saw her talking with my father-in-law, and she was so irritated. She looked at me and told me to go get the nurse. She wanted to go back in the ER, and she was trying to leave the room. I went to get the nurse and she came, and they moved her back, but something was different with her. I looked at Ma, and she looked at me. I knew that would be my last time seeing her. I walked out of the ER, and everyone was there—my whole family. As soon as the door closed, they called a code blue, and I asked the officer, "Was it the lady in pink?" and "You go check it out, please." And while he was walking, they called a code yellow. Shortly after, the officer came back and told me yes, she coded. I walked out of the ER and felt that Ma was gone. I felt her leaving me, and it felt like the umbilical cord was severally cut. I began to weep, then I looked up toward the sky and said, "Love you, Ma." I didn't want her to leave me alone here with these people. You see, my ma always had my back; she was always a fighter. No one messed with her kids, especially her second child. She loved all of us, but he was special, and everyone knew it because she would tell you so.

Crying and Dying Inside

I saw a shift in my personality after Ma died. It took something from me. I found myself wanting to be alone all the time. I stopped applying myself to any relationships; they didn't matter anymore. I found myself drifting away from my husband and my son. I fell into a rigorous work schedule. I made sure that I had no time for anyone. I hid my feeling inside of me because I couldn't trust anyone with them. The one person who knew me inside and out was gone. Who could help me now? Who could I trust now with all my secrets? I knew I was depressed, but I went to work smiling and laughing and acting like life was all good. I felt like no one could hear me crying inside. Wake up people, look at me. But no one did.

No Show

Why didn't my dad show up for my ma's home-going service? Why didn't my dad show up for his kids during their time of bereavement? I was so angry with him, so I carried that anger for over six years. Until one day.

T-19

I've got to go. I left the husband after years and years of just trying to fit a square peg in a round hole. It finally hit me that it would never work.

    I applied for an apartment and got it in two days. I went back out to 605 with a U-Haul truck and my youngest brother. It was time to leave for good. My brother helped me move into my first apartment. I was so excited about this but when night fall came reality set in, and I got scared. How did I get to this point again? Why am I going through another divorce with the same person again? Why didn't I notice his behavior before I married him again? Why did I get tricked again? Why did I allow him to make feel so stupid again? Why did I trust him again? I had so many questions. Questions that I had no answer to. But I was going to start peeling back the layers of this onion to see the real me.

My Rock

I know that after mom had passed granny was soon to follow, but my heart was not ready for it at all. My granny was and will always be my rock. She was my protector.

When I was young, I would grab the end of hold of her house dress and walk with her in the kitchen while she cooked, holding on and never letting go. My granny was a member of the Eastern Star and they always had card parties and get togethers at the house. We had the house with all the action all the time. Our front door stayed open even at 1505. I didn't have house keys until I was grown and moved out. There was always someone home, and you were never alone. My granny would go clean the White people's houses, and she would cook and clean and would still come home and take care of all of us.

Granny made sure we knew how to cook and clean house. She was also a cook at the diner at the Market off Florida Avenue. She was the jack of all trades and did it all. She was so sweet but don't get her wrong or you would feel her wrath and it was swift. Miss you granny.

Layers of Me

I was sleeping when I heard a voice that said, "God is trying to tell you something." I awoke the next day and called my youngest brother. I asked for our dad's phone number he gave it to me. I called my dad.

Once I spoke with him, I felt relieved because I was carrying this burden for many years, and I just had to let it go. Who knew I had so many layers to face about me? Who knew that I disguised the public man to protect the private man? Who knew that saving money for me wouldn't be easier than spending it? Who knew that my relationship with men stemmed from daddy issues? Who knew that I had to unpack layer after layer to discover myself? I haven't spoken to him in over six years. Nevertheless, I was armed with nothing but guilt. I called, he answered. I said, "Hello, Pop." He said, "Hello, my daughter." I began to cry. The first thing I asked him was if he knew who he was talking to, and he said, "Yes, my daughter." Then he asked me if I was back in church. I told him no. I was prepared to explain my story with a very lengthy explanation, but I paused and said no. I kept the conversation brief, then hung up.

Convicted

The next day my friend and I were heading toward Baltimore for a day of relaxation and fun, but to my dismay, we struck up a major conversation that changed our no-title-just-relations relationship upside down.

During the drive one of us started talking about religion in the car, and we got really quiet. He grew up in church and sang in the choir. I attended church with my godfather and granny while growing up. We never spoke of religion before, so I said that once we go down this road there is no turning back. The next week we got a referral to check out this amazing pastor at First Baptist Church of Glenarden in Upper Marlboro. I was hesitant because I haven't step foot inside of a church outside of all the funeral and wakes in 1980's.

My first visit there, I saw a big choir and people everywhere. We arrived for an 8 a.m. service. We came down to the fourth row from the pastor seat. The service began, and what an amazing service. I felt the Holy Spirit flowing all through the church and was getting excited and enjoying myself. until this older choir member began to sing.

"Touch the Hymn of his Garment." They were singing my granny's song. The last time I heard that song was when I was in church with her at the age of nineteen. I knew that this was meant to be, and that God was calling me back home. I began to cry so hard, and I was being convicted in my spirit. Then it was time for the word of God.

The service began, and the pastor was short in statute, but he also convicted me. He was on fire for the Lord. He convicted me, my lifestyle and my home arrangements. When Pastor gave the call to the altar, he specifically called for me when he said backsliders. I felt the Holy Spirit tell me I was doing the right thing. This was God's divine plan. I decided to get baptized again. This baptism would be so different this time because I would not be under distress. This baptism was what I wanted. During my baptism I believed the reverend held me down a little longer in the water so that my past sins would go away.

Go!

I signed up to take an Altar Counselor class in December of 2011. I heard a small voice inside of me that said, "Go." That voice never went away, and that was seven years ago.

On one Sunday morning we had a visiting pastor by the name of Tony Evans. Pastor Evans expounded on the scripture from Matthew 28:19. He explained what the word "go" means. The word "go" is a verb which means action. The word came from the Greek word Strong Concordance "porenomal"—to traverse, i.e., travel, depart, go, away forth, one's way make or take a journey, walk. I had an aha moment and know that I will exhort God's name on high. Every week after 8 a.m. or 10 a.m. service, I must "go" to the altar. God is calling me, and I am responding to His command and His will for my life.

Why Me!

I was invited to a discipleship program which I thought was a joke. I did accept the invitation and met with the group of women. The question which was posed to me was, "Why are you here?" I told them first, "I believe that this is a joke because I don't get along with women at all, and this might not work for me."

But deep down inside I knew who sent me: God. God can be such a big jokester at times. I did participate in the program and absolutely loved it. I was able to peel back the layers of me every week. Those women gave me the safety net and assured me that the room and the talks stayed confidential at all times. I felt so relieved that I was able to dump and leave it there weekly. I told them everything about me and my dreams and fears. I saw myself growing closer and closer to God weekly, and if that was the objective, they nailed it all the way. I am so grateful to those women and those moms who paved the way for me to walk through that valley of death and fear no evil. I love them, and I always will.

Jesus on the line

I knew in order to fulfill this call, I had to study the word of God. I began my journey down the ministerial track. I began to take several classes at church. These class would enhance my knowledge of God. These classes also allowed me to acknowledge my gifts.

I give credit to my Lord and Savior who has always been on my side through thick and thin. Everything I went through was a privilege and an honor. God is building my character piece by piece. My life is like a box of Legos—inside there are different shapes and sizes, and you can just make anything from a car to a skyscraper to a robot.

Preachin' Time

I was invited to preach at a Women's Conference in Northeast DC. I was so nervous I had no idea what I was going to say, and my thoughts were running crazy. I prayed and prayed, but nothing came to mind.

The scripture that came to mind was Matthew 28:18–20. In the same dream, I saw a piece of my granny's famous 5-5-5 cake. It was her famous pound cake. Whenever she made that cake, we would walk a mile to get a gallon of milk which paired well with the cake. This cake only had five ingredients, but only three main ingredients to make it work. I related these ingredients with having the Father, the Son, and the Holy Spirit, which I ran from for years. I never thought that God could use someone like me, a dressed- up trash can.

Renee R. White

This is only the beginning...

About the Author:

Renee R. White is a native of Washington, DC who grew up in the area called Uptown. She attended church weekly with her godfather at New Southern Rock Baptist Church. As a teenager, she attended Tried Stone Baptist Church with her grandmother, but left the church when she got pregnant. She can be found through her Facebook page: Renee R White.

www.ingramcontent.com/pod-product-compliance
Lightning Source LLC
LaVergne TN
LVHW051926060526
838201LV00062B/4712